MEDITATIONS
FOR A LESS STRESSFUL,
MORE AWESOME LIFE

STOP
breathe
CHILL

BETH STEBNER

D0032644

Aadamsmedia
AVON, MASSACHUSETTS

To Mike, Mom, and Dad.
Thanks for the loving reminders to live in the present.

Published by
Adams Media, a division of F+W Media, Inc.
57 Littlefield Street, Avon, MA 02322. U.S.A.
www.adamsmedia.com

ISBN 10: 1-4405-9439-2
ISBN 13: 978-1-4405-9439-7
eISBN 10: 1-4405-9443-0
eISBN 13: 978-1-4405-9443-4

Printed in the United States of America.

10 9 8 7 6 5 4 3 2 1

The information in this book should not be used for diagnosing or treating any health
problem. Not all diet and exercise plans suit everyone. You should always consult a
trained medical professional before starting a diet, taking any form of medication, or
embarking on any fitness or weight-training program. The author and publisher disclaim
any liability arising directly or indirectly from the use of this book.

Many of the designations used by manufacturers and sellers to distinguish their
products are claimed as trademarks. Where those designations appear in this book and
F+W Media, Inc. was aware of a trademark claim, the designations have been printed
with initial capital letters.

Cover design by Erin Alexander.
Cover image © iStockphoto.com/S-E-R-G-O.

This book is available at quantity discounts for bulk purchases.
For information, please call 1-800-289-0963.

CONTENTS

INTRODUCTION

If you're stressed out about an upcoming test, do you stay up late, binge on junk food, and snap at everyone around you as you frantically flip through your notes? If you have a blowup with a friend, do you avoid her at all costs instead of working things out? If you're single, do you find yourself jealous—like, really jealous—of other people's happy relationships? Do your parents' rules and never-ending questions about your life make you boil with rage?

Let's face it: Stress is everywhere you look. It's at school in the morning, hiding out in friendships, and is waiting for you every night when you get home. You can't avoid stress any more than you could avoid your own shadow—but you *can* control your reaction to it. Not only that, but you can learn how to deal with stress in a way that won't leave you feeling rotten, both inside and out. If you're turning to coffee, candy, all-nighters, and mental thunderstorms, you're only making your situation worse. This book will give you a different (and less candy-filled) way to approach stressful situations that actually *helps*.

Maybe you've heard of mindfulness from a magazine or TV show. Schools around the country—and maybe even yours—have started to incorporate it into daily routines. Perhaps your parents have even gotten into it. In its simplest form, mindfulness is the conscious awareness of what's happening right now, in this very moment. It's not thinking about what you're going to have for lunch in a few hours, or wondering if your friends are going to hang out without you this weekend. The practice of mindfulness can be applied to anything—if you're eating a meal and are aware of everything you're eating, that's mindful eating. In the same way, if you're doing your homework—yes, you do it mindfully, too! One way to practice mindfulness is through meditation, which celebrities from Emma Watson to Katy Perry practice. (You'll see that there are many simple ways to meditate—it doesn't have to mean sitting cross-legged on a mountaintop!) Mindfulness meditation is a way to approach stressful situations—big and small—in a calm, thoughtful way.

But mindfulness meditation isn't a one-time, cure-all magic bullet; it's a lifestyle, something you practice each and every day (like playing soccer or the clarinet). The more you practice it, the more natural it feels, and the more it can help you. Before you know it, you'll feel like your day isn't complete without sitting quietly to remind yourself of a favorite mantra!

This book will break down common stressful situations you probably encounter in your life, whether it's school stressors, relationship problems, issues with your best friend, doubts about your self-worth, or worries about the future. Then you'll learn ways that mindfulness meditation can help you deal with that particular scenario. Each entry wraps up with a mantra—a sentence or two that you can say out loud or in your head to remind yourself to be in the present moment. You can turn to these mantras whenever you need them, like right before a big test, or at the end of a stressful day before you go to bed. Once you remember to stop, breathe, relax, and chill, you're able to face your problem in a totally mindful way—and make your life happier, healthier, and less stressful.

"LIFE IS A DANCE.
MINDFULNESS
IS WITNESSING
THAT DANCE."

—AMIT RAY

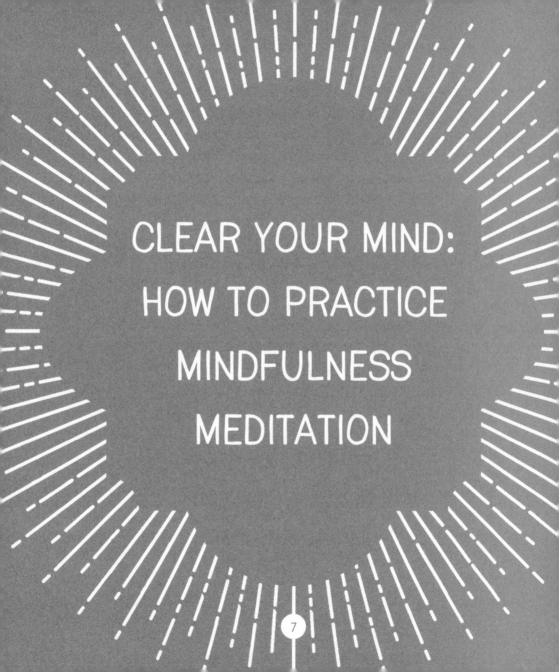

CLEAR YOUR MIND: HOW TO PRACTICE MINDFULNESS MEDITATION

If you think meditation is weird, boring, pointless, or only for hippies, think again. Meditating is an increasingly common (and popular!) way to insert a peaceful pause in your otherwise chaotic day, and you can literally do it anytime, anywhere. You don't have to be wearing any special clothes or playing any special music. (You'll probably discover certain preferences as you practice, though!) This chapter outlines the basics of how to start meditating.

STEP 1: STOP.

The first step in learning meditation is to *stop*. Yes, stop freaking out about your chemistry test, stop checking your Instagram feed, stop fuming about having to clean your room. Instead, set aside five minutes to devote to meditation, time that you would have otherwise wasted to fear, the bottomless hole that is the Internet, or anger. Set a reminder on your phone if you need to—and then put your phone away. Remember, there's no right way—and certainly no wrong way—to practice. The important thing to remember is to do it every day when you're starting out, preferably at the same time each day. Maybe in the morning before you go to school, or right before bed each night.

STEP 2: BREATHE.

Take a deep breath. Really deep. Did it feel strange? Like you maybe haven't taken a proper breath in a long time?

Odds are, you don't think too much about breathing most of the day (or at all), and that's because when you're focused on other tasks, the "control center" part of your brain goes on autopilot, sending signals that tell your lungs to inhale oxygen and exhale carbon dioxide and, you know, stay alive.

The "autopilot" breathing is shallow, the opposite of a "belly" breath that travels down your body and expands your ribcage. Belly breathing sends a message to your brain to let your body know, "Hey, Body, chill. Everything's cool here. We've got this." Deep breathing is the key to mindfulness meditation, as is reminding yourself to always be in the present and observe it without judgment or additional thought.

Think of it this way: Breathing is the first thing you do when you're born. It's the last thing you'll do in your lifetime. Your breathing is the thread that weaves together the tapestry of your life. When you breathe, you can only do it in the present. You can't go back and breathe differently in the past, and you can't hoard future breaths. You only have this present moment. That's why breathing is so important to mindfulness. We'll get more into breathing later on in the book, too.

STEP 3: CHILL.

For your first meditation, try sitting in whatever way you find comfortable. If that means sitting cross-legged on a mat, fine, but you could just be sitting on a park bench or in your parked car. Keep your eyes open and remember, this is just a trial run. Start breathing deeply, gently letting your mind focus on your breath. If your thoughts wander, don't worry about it! Gently remind yourself to go back to thinking about the present and focusing on your breath. Forgive yourself for letting your thoughts meander, and withhold any judgment that you're not "doing it right."

In this first meditation, don't worry about incorporating a mantra or go in with the expectation of wanting to come out on the other side calmer and totally enlightened (trust me on this; meditation is a practice, not a thing to perfect!). Try imagining your thoughts as a stream, and you watch them trickle by as you sit by the water's edge. As your thoughts flow by, simply visualize watching them. If you start obsessing over one thought, reset yourself and try again. This will take time, but it's important not to get frustrated. You'll get the hang of it!

Another approach is counting slowly from one to ten as you breathe in and out, inhaling on the odd numbers and exhaling on the even ones. This gives your brain purpose without having to focus so heavily on simply observing thoughts. And again, if you start playing a thought or memory on repeat, just start back at one.

Try meditating for five minutes to start, and gradually build up your time. Notice how you're feeling. Are you more peaceful inside, your mind more like a calm lake? Or does your mind still feel like an ocean during a storm? How does your body feel? Are your muscles less tense and more relaxed, or are you still holding tension in your shoulders and neck? If you still feel a bit overwhelmed or tense, that's okay. Remember, this is a process—a journey to chill, if you will—not a sprint. The more you practice, the better it will work.

When you feel up for it, find specific mantras and scenarios in this book that will help you stay focused on the present that you can repeat to yourself. Ready? Great! Let the journey to the here and now begin!

"FRIENDSHIP IS BORN AT
THAT MOMENT WHEN ONE
MAN SAYS TO ANOTHER:
'WHAT! YOU TOO?
I THOUGHT THAT NO ONE
BUT MYSELF. . . .'"

—C.S. LEWIS

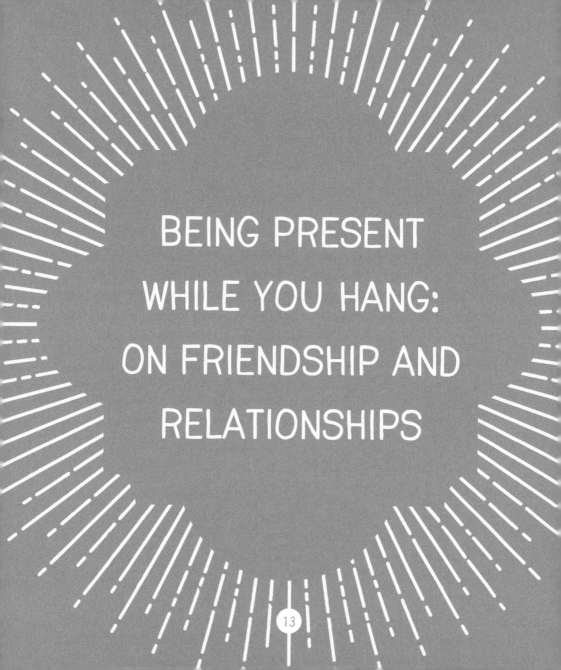

BEING PRESENT
WHILE YOU HANG:
ON FRIENDSHIP AND
RELATIONSHIPS

BE THE KIND OF *friend* YOU'D WANT TO HAVE

Friends make bad days better, give you someone to talk with or text after class, and help you make hilarious memories that will last a lifetime. Plus, they can tell you if you've been walking around with toilet paper stuck to your shoe or broccoli in your teeth because, hey, we've all been there. But maintaining a friendship takes time and effort, and to have friends, you first have to be the kind of person that will attract them. Yeah, okay; but how do you do that? Think of what traits and qualities you want in a friend—maybe someone who's fiercely loyal or who is a good listener—and try to practice those traits in all your relationships.

Friendship is a reflection of who I am, so to have friends, I need to be a friend first.

HOW TO *listen* TO A FRIEND

On your mission to be a good friend, it's important to remember that everyone is dealing with *something*. Maybe it's a bad grade in biology; maybe there's trouble at home. So if one of your friends seems "off," ask if you can do anything to help that person and see what happens. Just being there to listen—not even to offer a solution, but to really just sit down and *listen* without checking your phone or looking around to see if your other friends are nearby—is incredibly kind and meaningful. As the old saying goes, "A friend in need is a friend indeed!" Be that friend, indeed.

In order to hear, I must listen. Listening is the way to understanding, and will help me on the path to true friendship.

DON'T *be* A BAD FRIEND

Good friends listen to your problems; they're there for you, and are lifesavers in a pinch. But not every friend is a good one. Think of someone who might be a "bad" friend. Does she always talk about her own accomplishments and never ask questions about you? Does it seem like he's only seeking validation or attention from you with no intention of giving back? Everyone's capable of slipping into the "bad" friend territory—all it takes is a hectic sports schedule or a stressful class for you to morph from friend of the millennium to self-absorbed narcissist. The key is being mindful of your *friends'* needs, not just your own. Do they need to vent about something? Hang out? Could you support their efforts by going to watch their play, hockey game, or debate? Being in tune with your friends ensures that you don't drift apart.

My friendships are precious like silver, and sometimes they need some polish. I will put in the effort to make sure my friendships don't get tarnished.

ON *being* COMPASSIONATE

There's an old Sanskrit word, *maitrī*, which, loosely translated, means "unconditional friendship" or "unconditional compassion." It could mean unconditional friendship with yourself (more on that in the Self-Esteem and Self-Care chapter), but the idea can also be applied to friendship with those around you and wishing them well in their own lives. Being compassionate could simply be thinking of a friend going through a tough time and feeling warmth and compassion for him or her. Sending good vibes to people while you meditate is a great way to keep positive energy around them—and you.

With warmth, compassion, and empathy, I think of others and actively wish them well.

WHEN YOU AND YOUR BEST FRIEND *fight*

If you're at the beach for a week, odds are that there will probably be some beautiful, sunny days, but also one or two rainy ones. Friendship is kind of like the weather, and you'll deal with your fair share of storms. You and your BFF *will* fight at some point. Maybe over an incident at school, maybe over a crush. But there's hope. In a recent study, psychologists from Wilfrid Laurier University found that friends who knew each other's "triggers," or things that set them off, were less likely to fight. So if you know your friend freaks out when you don't return clothes you borrowed in a timely manner, you might try to avoid that situation by returning her stuff right after you use it. So while some fights may be inevitable, keep them few and far between by thinking of your friend's triggers, and above all, keep your cool. The storm will eventually blow over.

Fighting is temporary and part of any friendship. I can weather this storm and I'll come out stronger than before.

WHEN YOUR BEST FRIEND ISN'T
your BEST FRIEND ANYMORE

Not all friendships stand the test of time. It's perfectly natural for you and your besties from elementary school to grow apart as you get older. They may end up liking video games and computers, while you become more interested in theater. That's okay. Pursuing different interests doesn't make you a bad person! But it's important to treat your old BFFs with kindness and not punish them for wanting to pursue other things or make other friends, even though you may feel like you've been abandoned (not to mention promises of being friends forever being broken). If you go to the same school, try to make a little time in your day to catch up and see what they've been up to (remember, listening is super important!). If you've moved on to different schools, go beyond social media and meet up IRL if it feels right. It can be good to hold on to people from your past, but moving on is totally healthy, too.

With growth comes change.
With change comes wisdom.
With wisdom comes understanding
and the ability to move on.

RECONNECT WITH AN *old* FRIEND

Sometimes, people grow apart. Maybe you had a friend from kindergarten with whom you were inseparable. You were partners in crime on the playground, ate lunch together every day, and spent countless hours at each other's houses after school. But then you grew apart, for whatever reason. The great thing is, it's never too late to reconnect with your pal, and odds are that he or she has thought about you just as much but didn't know how to make the first steps. Try dropping a line on social media or shooting an e-mail to an old friend, making sure to include a mention of one of your fond memories together. Old friendships can definitely be worth pursuing, and you'll be glad you put the time in.

Reaching out to a friend from
the past, I cultivate a friend
for the future.

WHEN YOUR FRIENDS *gang up* AGAINST YOU

At one point in the movie *Mean Girls*, Lindsay Lohan's character, Cady, pits all of the Plastics against each other, only to have everyone turn on *her*. Sometimes that happens in real life, too, and friends gang up on you—either fairly or unfairly. Since you look to your friends to be your biggest support system, this situation is really stressful! There's no cut-and-dried answer for how to solve a problem like this, but it's best to start by looking inward—have you been acting in a way that might cause your friends to behave this way toward you? Talking to your friends calmly can help clear up misunderstandings. Remember, try not to let your anger, jealously, or hurt get in the way.

I am calm and in control,
and will use love to seek
out answers.

DEALING WITH *Loneliness* AND FEELING LEFT OUT

When you're constantly surrounded by classmates, teammates, and family, it's hard to grasp that in the midst of all those people you can still feel lonely and alone. Combine that with a bombardment of advertisements and Instagram feeds showing people having endless hours of fun with their seemingly perfect friends and Girl Squads, and it's hard not to feel like everyone else is having the time of their lives—everyone except you. But the truth is, almost everyone feels left out at one point or another. It's human nature to want to belong, but everyone deals with periods of feeling excluded and lonesome. Remember that neither of these situations shows your full reality, and you're in charge of how you feel.

Loneliness is just a feeling, like any other. When I look inside me, I find happiness and fulfillment, light and joy. I use these feelings to fill me up with happiness, driving my loneliness away.

HOW TO *travel* WITH FRIENDS

Going on vacation with a friend is great. It's exciting! You're off to see the world! Finally, you've got the chance to explore a new place and have adventures away from your hometown. You'll also likely be sharing very close quarters with your friend (or friends) for long stretches of time if you're traveling by plane, train, or car. In fact, a lot of travel is actually pretty exhausting and stressful, from time spent in transit to decisions about what to do when you get there. Lost luggage? Stressful. Money issues? Stress to the max. A clingy friend? Not exactly a walk on the beach. Remember to take each experience as it comes. Sometimes, the best part of the trip can be a *mis*adventure you and your friend have. Another thing to keep in mind: Just because you're on vacation together doesn't mean you have to be attached at the hip. Give your friends space and alone time if they need it and it's safe to do so. And give yourself some, too! Hey, you're on vacation!

I'm lucky to be able to share a
new place with a good friend
and keep my heart and mind
open to new experiences,
whatever they may be.

SHOULD YOU *try* TO BE POPULAR?

As long as there have been schools (the first American school was founded in Boston around 1635, BTW), there have been the popular kids—impossibly cooler, thinner, more beautiful, and more interesting than you think you'll ever be. But here's a secret: These kids are just as insecure as you are, in need of reassurance that they're loved and accepted. But sometimes, they have less-than-great ways of showing it. They might make fun of your clothes or your hair, or say mean things on social media. Or they might not pay any attention to you whatsoever. The trick to dealing with not-so-nice popular kids is to realize not everyone in the world is going to like you (even though you're probably very likable!) and that it's usually a waste of time to try to win their affection. Instead, focus on being positive and maintaining your own meaningful friendships. Realize that other classmates are likely feeling the same way you are. Being popular is transient, but being a good friend is a lasting goal.

Worrying about how other people perceive me is a poor use of my time. I will focus my time and energy on being a good friend.

MANTRA
~ 35 ~

Loving COMPLETELY

Think about how you use the word "love." You "love" that new leather jacket you saw on Pinterest, or you "loved" that new song by your favorite singer. But to love completely? That's a different level of love. It means putting your pride on hold and opening yourself up, making yourself vulnerable (which is a totally scary yet invigorating idea!). Loving someone completely—a friend or a parent, for instance—requires you to be completely present for another person, accepting this person's flaws, quirks, and, yes, sometimes even his or her smelly feet. This type of love doesn't have to be romantic at all—it could be as simple as being there for a friend in need, showing your parents you love them and appreciate them, and allowing yourself to be loved in return.

When I allow myself to love completely, I open myself up to new experiences, and in return open myself up to be loved.

BE *present* DURING DATES

So, you've done it. You've either asked someone out on a date (go you!) or have been asked out (still; go you!). Now what? Yes, there's the requisite scramble for what to do. (Hot tip: Don't overthink it. A movie and a milkshake is timeless. Or make it a coffee, if that's your thing.) But in between the movie and the macchiato, don't forget the reason *why* the date is happening in the first place—you and the other person are exploring a connection, so the date is really about finding out more about each other. Having a meaningful discussion is hard enough without either of you scrolling through Facebook, Twitter, Instagram, and Snapchat every other minute. As hard as it is, put your phone away. Learn to be present and enjoy the ambiance of the coffee shop or restaurant. Take in the music, the feel of the sofa, the sound of your date's voice, and listen to what your date has to say. The first step to a real connection is making sure that connection actually happens.

Many things in life deserve my attention, especially when it comes to friends and dating. I will be present in the moment and learn to let go of distractions.

ACTUALLY HAVE *fun* ON YOUR DATE!

It goes without saying that dates should be fun—otherwise, what's the point? Don't get hung up on microanalyzing everything your date does and worrying that he or she may be having a bad time. Try letting go of expectations and just enjoy your date's company. It's not a job interview or some sort of test; it's a way to get to know someone else. So take your nervous energy and channel it into something productive—like a thoughtful question about the person's interests. Or an idea for a second date!

The only person who puts expectations on me is myself. I will let go of these pressures and remember to have fun in the moment.

HOW TO DEAL WITH A *broken* HEART

As much as you hope your relationship will last forever (or at least for the foreseeable future), things happen. Dating in middle school and high school is an imperfect art. Think of how bad you were at spelling when you started kindergarten, and how much better at it you are now. It's the same with relationships. With age and time, you'll simply get better at them—including dealing with heartbreak. Whether or not things ended on good terms, keep in mind that as much as things hurt now, the pain will get better in time. Focus on the good parts of your relationship and how you two helped each other grow. It's not easy, but reflecting—and eventually moving on—will help you grow.

Heartache, though painful,
can help me grow as a person.
I will explore how I feel and
remember that, with time,
the pain will pass.

BE *mindful* OF YOUR SINGLE FRIENDS

It's really difficult when your friend starts dating someone new and exciting, like the football quarterback or the lead of the school play. You feel like an afterthought because suddenly your friend and confidante is nothing more than a casual acquaintance who says loudly as she passes you in the hall that she "can't wait to hang out!" But how should you act if *you're* on the other side, and you've just started going out with someone new? Imagine how your friend feels now that you're not spending as much time together. Maybe he's lonely? Maybe she feels resentful about this new person who displaced your already-chill group dynamic. Be mindful of their feelings and make an effort to keep your friendships going strong by keeping them in the loop, inviting them to group activities (there's nothing worse than hearing "We didn't think you'd want to come because it was just couples"), and planning some all-important one-on-one bonding time.

Just because my relationship status has changed doesn't mean my friendship status has to. Neither is mutually exclusive, and I will think of how to keep my friendships strong with my single friends.

APPRECIATE THE *good* RELATIONSHIPS IN YOUR LIFE

Throughout the day, it's easy to get caught up in whatever is going on. A geometry test. A pop quiz in history (Oh no! Where *didn't* Napoleon conquer?). But in the midst of the chaos is the constant stream of positive people in your life. Your relationships—whether romantic or platonic—are some of the most important things in your life outside of your family. Remind yourself to take time out of the day to reflect on these people and what they mean to you. Couldn't get through the day without texting one of your friends? Let him know. Love spending time with another friend studying for Spanish exams? Tell her! And *en español,* if you can.

Mindfulness is as much about being conscious of the here and now as it is reflecting on the things that are important in your life. So why not take that one step further and tell these superstars how much they mean to you. It'll brighten their day and make you that much more thankful.

I'm constantly thankful for all the good people in my life.

IF HE (OR SHE) DOESN'T *like* YOU BACK

If you've ever taken a poetry or English class, odds are that you've read a poem describing the agony of loving someone who doesn't love you back. There's no way around it—loving someone who doesn't feel the same way is the worst. But it's not the end of the world. Just because someone doesn't like you back doesn't mean you're not worthy of being liked (or loved). The best thing you can do is realize that there are a number of factors at play—maybe she likes someone else, maybe he has no idea you actually like him—and move on. That could mean hanging out more with friends, picking up a new hobby, or working on a self-improvement project (like meditation!).

Just because someone doesn't love me doesn't mean I'm unlovable. I am an interesting, engaging person worthy of love that will find me when the time is right.

FIGURING OUT WHO YOU *really* LIKE

When you're in your teens, your brain is constantly changing and grow-ing as you slowly turn into an adult. Think of it kind of like a really com-plicated city being built one spiraling skyscraper at a time. There's a lot going on, and a lot to try out. One day, you might go for someone in the popular crowd; the next, it's the brooding artist. The beauty of being young is you have time to figure out yourself and who you are as a person. Figuring out what motivates and inspires you is a huge first step. Think of people you could see yourself getting along with. Who makes you laugh? Who's fun to be around? Don't focus *just* on looks—trust me on this one; that's a one-way ticket to disappointment.

Being honest and clear,
I will think of the traits and
values that are attractive
to me and use those to
help me choose who I want
to spend time with.

accepting OTHERS

It's so important to accept others the way they are. Whether they look different than you, come from a different background or religion, whether their parents are rich or not, no matter if they like boys or girls—everyone deserves to be loved. It's a basic human principle, and the sooner you learn it, the better off you'll be. Approach peoples' differences with friendly curiosity, not judgment, sarcasm, and especially not taunting or bullying. Bullies are afraid of things they don't understand and make other people feel bad about things they can't change. The more you try to understand where other people are coming from, the better your life will be. And remember: Before you can really accept yourself, you have to be accepting of others, no matter what their background or beliefs.

Acceptance of others is key to my acceptance of self.

KNOW YOUR *worth*

There's an old quote by Eleanor Roosevelt that's helpful in nearly any aspect of your life, whether it's dating rejection, trouble in school, or a big brother making you feel lousy about yourself: "No one can make you feel inferior without your consent." To translate? You're in control of your feelings, no one else. And the former First Lady was on to something profound. You are very, very worth it and valued, which is a pretty powerful thought. The realization that you have total control over your feelings is comforting in many situations. And no one—not the person you're dating, not a family member, not a teacher—can take that away from you.

No one can make me feel inferior without my consent, and anyone who tries is not worth my time and energy.

R-E-S-P-E-C-T!

Respecting other people seems like Common Courtesy 101, but it isn't always. And we're not talking about just holding doors or saying "please" or "thank you." Respect for another person means respecting his or her boundaries. If you're texting your girlfriend and she doesn't immediately respond, keep your cool and respect her space—there are any number of reasons why she may be incommunicado. A teacher or parent could have confiscated the phone, she could have forgotten it in study hall, her battery might have kicked the bucket. Respect extends way beyond texting, of course—it's a way of life that helps pass along positive energy. In a way, it's really just another way to think about being mindful of other people.

Being respectful is like being mindful. I choose to treat people in my life as equals and with respect.

"A HAPPY FAMILY
IS BUT AN EARLIER
HEAVEN."

—GEORGE BERNARD SHAW

MINDFULNESS
AT HOME:
FAMILY AND SPACES

HOW TO *deal* WITH HELICOPTER PARENTS

Call it what you will—lawnmower parents, bulldozer parents, or the more popular helicopter parents—these are moms and dads (or other loved ones) who hover over your every move, often doing things that you as a responsible teenager could do just as easily (your own laundry, class projects, buttering your toast in the morning). While all these actions usually come from a place of love (yes, your parents want you to succeed!), it can be overwhelming to deal with the incessant supervision and fussing. Try having a talk with your parents to understand their point of view. Let them know you appreciate the help, but you need to branch out on your own. Here's some helpful adult advice: If you forget your homework or your lunch money, you need to face the music, not have your parents hovering around to save the day.

My parents want what's best for me and my future. Using that power, I'll propel myself to greatness.

ASKING FOR MORE *support*
FROM YOUR PARENTS

Some parents are very busy and are always bouncing from one thing to the next. Maybe they have a really demanding job, or take care of other family members. Either way, they're missing out on soccer games, PTA meetings, math competitions, and your debut in the school play. Whatever the case, remember that despite their time crunch, your parents love you. It's always worth sitting them down to talk about what your needs are. Maybe they can try to rearrange a meeting or have someone record your performance so they can watch it later. If you don't speak up, you'll never get what you hope for.

I am a capable person worthy
of support, and will ask for it as
often as I need it.

WHEN YOU'VE BEEN GROUNDED *unfairly*

Hate to break it to you, but parents are always on high alert for signs of misbehavior or disobedience, *especially* with teenagers. Sometimes you don't deserve a punishment because a) your sister did it and framed you so she'd escape a grounding, or b) there was just an honest misunderstanding. Realizing that your parents aren't perfect or omniscient will help you out a whole lot here. Yes, you can argue your case calmly and logically—it's good to speak up for yourself—but if the punishment isn't severe and you've only lost TV privileges for a day and kept your sister out of trouble, maybe that's not the worst. Besides, you can use that downtime away from the TV to catch up on your meditation. Or anything else, really.

Learning to be a forgiving, understanding person is a pursuit worthy of my time.

WHEN YOU'VE BEEN GROUNDED FOR A
good REASON

Sometimes, you mess up and have to suffer the consequences. This is actually a good thing, because the whole point of being punished is to let you know that your privileges, whether it's having a smartphone or being able to stay out late, are in fact privileges, not rights. Try to think of the time while you're grounded as a prime time for mindfulness, where you focus on what you did wrong, how it potentially hurt other people, how you *won't* do it again, and how you can be better in the future. And just because something was taken away from you (like a computer or smartphone), you don't have to feel bored and resentful. Try discovering a new hobby, writing down your feelings, or even picking up a book.

No one is perfect, and being grounded is a time to reflect on how I can be better.

WHY YOU'RE *fighting* WITH YOUR SIBLINGS (AND HOW TO STOP!)

Sometimes you might feel as though your brothers and sisters were put on this planet solely to annoy you and get you grounded, setting traps for you at every turn and waiting for you to screw up. After all, it's not called "sibling rivalry" for nothing, and the saying "familiarity breeds contempt" can also be uncomfortably true. You compete with your siblings for attention and space, for starters. Who gets more time with Mom and Dad? Who gets the bigger bedroom? But look at it this way—your siblings are uniquely yours, and together, you make up a family. If you look at living with your siblings like a team sport where you all have to work together, versus an every-man-for-himself competition, the sailing will be a lot smoother and more harmonious.

There's no one else in the world like a brother or sister. I will be present when I'm with mine and learn to ask questions, hear what they have to say, and realize that differences help us all grow.

IF YOUR *family* IS GROWING

Families are always changing and growing. If your parents have just told you that you're about to become a big brother or big sister, it's time to get excited about helping to care for a new life. Or maybe one of your parents is remarrying and some stepbrothers or stepsisters are entering the equation. Sure, it might be foreign and more than a little strange to think that soon your family will have a new member(s), but there is a lot of fun in store. Remember that every moment with your siblings—new, old, step, or half—is precious. There is no cookie-cutter family, no right or wrong size or makeup. So find a way to celebrate that, and embrace being a part of a truly modern family.

Families come in all shapes and sizes. No matter who enters mine, I'll treat them with love and respect.

MOVING TO A *new* PLACE

In the Pixar flick *Inside Out*, Riley's family relocates from the Midwest to San Francisco, uprooting the preteen from a life full of hockey games and friends to a cramped apartment and uncertainty. Moves are stressful, but it's all about how you frame it. We learned (rather beautifully) in *Inside Out* that it's okay to be sad and that it's possible to feel a mixture of complex emotions all at once. Once you've moved, focus on all of the things you're thankful for at the new place. Is the weather sunnier and warmer? Are you closer to some family members than you were before? Does your house have more space or a bigger backyard? Centering your thoughts on the positive will help you deal better with any negative feelings you may have.

Moving to a different place gives me the opportunity to discover new things around me. My heart is open, my feet are ready to explore, my mind is ready to learn.

MANTRA
∿ 73 ∿

WHEN *parents* JUST DON'T UNDERSTAND

If your parents had you in their twenties or thirties, they're nearly two decades behind what is cool or on trend (which could help explain their perplexing fashion choices). Even their language for describing what's cool probably sounds retro. The point is, when you're a teenager, there are going to be times when—thanks to a nifty generational gap—your parents won't understand why it was so soul crushing when your favorite band broke up or why you need to have pink—sorry, rose gold—hair. Your parents are allowed to be clueless about fads, even though it probably makes you squirm when your dad tries to talk cool with your friends. But remember—they're doing this from a place of love, and your mom's fashion sense (or lack thereof) isn't what's important. It's their love for you that matters most. In fact, if you were able to look ten years ahead to the future, it wouldn't matter at all.

My parents may not understand everything I like, but they love me, and life is more important than just appearances.

IF YOU *need* MORE BOUNDARIES FROM YOUR PARENTS

Maybe it started early. You would go to the grocery store with your parents as a young child and see a sweet cereal you absolutely *had* to have. You begged, you pleaded, you goaded, and—you got what you wanted. But small treats and indulgences when you were a kid led to bigger leniencies, and bigger concessions. Homework? Nah, don't worry about it. You can stay out as late as you want. Getting everything you want all the time—or having parents that don't set boundaries— seems like a teenager's dream, but it's an illusion. Believe it or not, that nagging and pestering and checking in exists for a reason: To help you learn what's right and wrong and how to make good decisions. If you yearn for more rules, it never hurts to ask for them or tell your parents how you're feeling. Beyond that, realize that nothing in life is perfect and, hard as it may be to understand, you will learn a lot from setting your own boundaries.

Creating boundaries is a way to create harmony. Structure exists to make life more balanced.

DECLUTTERING YOUR *space*

It's funny to think about how much stuff we accumulate over time: Shoes. Clothes. Computers. Games. Gadgets. Smartphones. Books (well, sometimes). Old school notes. Sports gear. Souvenirs. Birthday presents and cards from family members, including that itchy sweater that you're forced to wear at Christmas. And the list goes on and on. Your stuff is an extension of who you are, and there's a huge amount of comfort to being surrounded by it. But it doesn't define who you are. When you're looking at a room full of clutter, you're looking at total chaos!

Marie Kondo, author of *The Life-Changing Magic of Tidying Up*, has a simple yet genius solution—ask yourself if a particular item gives you joy. If not, get rid of it (or donate it!). You'll find that you really don't need all of the stuff you think you do, and your mind will thank you for the obvious lack of clutter.

Objects in my life should bring me joy. A cluttered space leads to a cluttered mind.

ON DOING *chores*

Let's be real, chores are the worst. Those dirty pots and pans taunt you from miles away, reminding you that you can't really relax until they're sitting spick-and-span in the cabinets. But studies have shown that doing chores—especially starting to do them at an early age—is good for everyone in the house. According to Marty Rossmann, a professor emeritus at the University of Minnesota, kids who were given chores early in life—around four years old—had a more solid relationship with their parents. But wait, there's more! These grocery-helping, floor-sweeping, lawn-mowing wunderkinds were also found to be self-sufficient and had better grades. So rather than think of chores as, well, a chore, think of them as the ultimate exercise in mindfulness—using time to reflect and meditate. And maybe, just maybe, the chores won't seem so daunting.

Chores and cleaning are just another way for me to practice mindfulness. The time spent doing them is sacred time, carved out just for me. It is my time, and I will use it fully.

THE *pros* OF HELPING OUT AROUND THE HOUSE (NO, REALLY!)

Chores are one thing, but being helpful around the house is the next level. Think of the former as homework that is expected no matter what, and the latter as extra credit that will earn you major points. It goes beyond just doing laundry and taking out the trash, and heads into the territory of being the greatest kid your parents could ever ask for. How can you be helpful around the house? Anticipate their needs. If you see that you're running low on dish soap or garbage bags and you can get to the store easily, buy some. If it's not your turn to do laundry but you see a big load of sheets that needs washing, wash and fold away. You'll be doing your parents a huge favor, and as an added bonus, being so proactive often has the fringe benefit of getting your mom and dad to ease up on being helicopter parents and micromanaging. When you prove you're responsible and thoughtful, only good things can come of it.

Being aware of all that is around me, I will anticipate what I can do to make life easier for the people I love.

A *clean* ROOM IS WORTH THE HASSLE

Picture this: You're up at 4 A.M. for swim practice and have to head straight from school to a swim meet, followed by study group for your upcoming math test. And you have a book report due tomorrow, too. In the midst of all of this, it's easy to forget that your bedroom chair isn't actually your closet, your towel shouldn't live on the floor, and the kitchen isn't a landing spot for unwashed dishes. But something has to give, doesn't it? Not necessarily. Try waking up just ten or fifteen minutes earlier (ugh, I know!) to pay some attention to your room—quickly put away your socks, make sure your towel is hung so it won't start to get all mildew-y and gross. While it may be painful to hear the alarm so early, remember that the peace you'll find coming home to a neat room is worth it (especially when you can find your socks).

Taking time to organize will add order and structure to my life.

CREATING A *chill* SPOT IN YOUR ROOM

Your room is probably where you spend a lot of your time when you're home. You sleep there, your clothes are stored there (hopefully in closets or drawers, not the floor), and the rest of your stuff is there too. You probably use your room as a space to do homework or hang out with friends. But all that stuff and—dare we say, clutter—could be distracting. Sure, it's good to put things away and have a space free of untidiness and dirty underwear, but try taking it one step further. Pick a corner of your room that you can use as a place to meditate and feel calm. It should be away from electronics like your TV or computer and other distractions. You don't need much—just a pillow or a rug— to make it your meditation space. Use your time in your meditation spot to center yourself and breathe, and feel totally cool, calm, and collected.

My space is my own, and surrounding myself with calm tranquility leads to peace.

THE *great* OUTDOORS

When was the last time you stopped to look at a tree, or even stopped to smell the roses? Your only contact with nature shouldn't be the ocean-scented hand soap in your bathroom. Give yourself time to go outside as much as you can, and enjoy being out there. Bring a book or a magazine to read, write in a journal, or just hang out with a friend in your backyard. Even if you live in a big city, there are plenty of parks where you can appreciate flowers and trees. Make sure to focus on the sound of the wind rustling the leaves, the way the sun dances through the canopy, and the birdsong around you. It's more restorative than you might think, and a great way to calm an overburdened mind.

Pursuing serene moments in nature, I take in the beauty and calm around me.

"ANY FOOL CAN KNOW.
THE POINT IS TO
UNDERSTAND."

—ALBERT EINSTEIN

KEEP CALM

AND STUDY ON:

SCHOOL

91

STARTING A *new* SCHOOL

Picture this: Your mom or dad gets a new job in an unfamiliar city, meaning that you and your siblings have to move with them (maybe even across the country) and enroll in a new school, leaving behind your old classmates, friends, and teachers. Stepping through the doors for the first time is incredibly nerve-wracking, and you probably feel angry at your parents for uprooting you from a familiar place. Instead of fuming at them, try to see it in a positive light. You have the chance to meet a whole new group of people and live in a new part of the state (or country!). Keep yourself open to new possibilities and friendships, and you'll keep yourself on the path to success.

I am intelligent, capable, and strong, and can handle any obstacle put before me.

COMMUTING *mindfully*

Getting to and from school every day can be a drag. Maybe your parents drive you, or you carpool with a sibling. Or you might take the bus, or maybe the subway. But any way you travel, you have to do it twice a day, for every school day of the year. That's a lot of back and forth—and a lot of opportunities to focus on the here and now. Instead of zoning out or staring at your phone, focus on how you're feeling. Tired? Elated? If you're walking, consciously notice how your body feels (see Mindfulness on Foot in the Self-Esteem and Self-Care chapter for more on mindful walking). Now, take a look at your surroundings and observe everything outside the car, bus, or subway. Are there a lot of trees? Buildings? Now, focus on the sounds around you. Maybe it's your friends chatting happily behind you on the bus or your big brother singing along to the radio, or maybe you hear the sound of rain hitting the windshield. By being present, you're helping your mind focus and making every single commute something new and different.

Using my senses, I see, hear,
and feel everything around me.

HOW TO PAY *attention* IN CLASS

At some point, even the most interesting subjects can sound boring and unintelligible and your favorite teacher no more engrossing than the sound of an old vacuum cleaner. Unfortunately, you still have to figure out how to pay attention (your grade depends on it, after all!). There are a ton of tips and tricks to doing this—for instance, you can sit in the front row so you are forced to pay attention and can't start daydreaming. Raise your hand often to answer questions, and make sure to sit far away from the class clown, since the joker's constant commentary makes it easy to get sucked into thinking that the class is stupid and doesn't matter. Even playing a game where you challenge yourself to take the most detailed notes possible will help, since you're competing against the toughest critic you know—yourself.

My attention is my own, and
I will call it to my use in and out
of class. The only one who loses
when I zone out is me.

HOW TO *focus* ON A LONG-TERM PROJECT

Odds are, at some point in your life, you've been assigned a long-term project like a book report, a presentation, or a term paper that requires days (if not weeks) of researching and collaborating with your classmates. And while it probably feels pretty good to throw the deadlines for those projects into a forgotten corner and enjoy your free time, that has been scientifically proven *not* to help in the long run. Being mindful of deadlines is the best way to tackle any large assignment, and stops you from becoming panicked or overwhelmed. Look at how much time you have to complete the assignment, then write down the steps you'll need to take to reach your goals. If you're working on a term paper on FDR and have a month to do it, start as soon as you receive the assignment, making an outline, doing research, and keeping track of what you still have to check off the list. Planning your time means you'll ultimately have much less stress when your project is finally due.

Time only moves forward, so
I will make sure to use my time
in such a way that I won't regret
looking back.

HEAR, HEAR! HOW TO BE A *better* LISTENER

Remember the last time you tried to open up to your best friend—only to see her tapping away at her phone? Or when your parents are telling you about how your cousins are and your eyes glaze over? Or when you were listening to your teacher explain something but not really digesting the words? *Hearing* something isn't the same as really *listening*, and today there are more distractions than ever. Being a good listener presents a set of challenges, but you can overcome them. If you're distracted by social media when your friend is trying to tell you about his day, make a rule that you can only use your phone when no one is speaking to you. Or if you find yourself tuning your parents out, try paraphrasing what they're saying back to them—"Oh, so my cousin Lisa is starting college next year?"—and follow up with another question like, "Does she know what she'll major in?" In class, take notes to be sure you can capture what's being taught in your own words. Being a better listener is a fantastic (and necessary) skill to have at every point in your life; the more you show you can listen, the better off you'll be.

Truly listening to what others have to say helps me live in the moment.

MASTER *public* SPEAKING

It's the moment every student dreads—that time when the teacher calls you to the front of the class to deliver a book report or a presentation. Your palms are sweaty, your knees are shaking, and your mouth suddenly feels like cotton. You're terrified that you've forgotten all of your talking points, and your mind goes blank. This is a totally natural reaction to a high-stress situation, but that doesn't make it any more fun. The best thing you can do is practice. Plus, think of it this way—all of your classmates eventually have to have their turn and speak, right? And they're probably just as nervous as you. Don't try the age-old tip of picturing the audience in their underwear (trust me, this will only make you giggle); instead, take calm, centering breaths. Look around for familiar faces that could help encourage you as you go, and get ready. Draw your shoulders back, straighten your notes, smile. You're prepared, you're poised. And you've totally got this.

I'm happy to be here, and
the knowledge I share will be
useful and interesting.

STUDYING *over* SNAPCHATTING

The draw of social media is—to put it mildly—irresistible. Study after study has shown that the more you use your smartphone, the more you *want* to use it. One study reported on CNN found that teens who were most active on social media checked their social networks more than 100 times a day. Clearly, it is super hard to just put your phone down and be present. When you have a big test to study for, try making these rules: Give your phone to a sibling or parent and tell that person you can't have it back until you've read through your homework for the night or memorized material for a big test. Or, if you think you have more willpower, try simply shutting your phone down for a few hours so you're not tempted to check what that buzz or ding was.

Focusing my attention on the task in front of me, I center my thoughts and tune all else out.

TEST PREP *101*

If the acronyms SAT or ACT strike fear into your very being, you dread the upcoming proficiency test, or you've ever sat at your desk with a blank exam because you just can't seem to get your brain into gear, don't worry! Tests, like anything else in life, require preparation. You wouldn't compete in a soccer tournament without having practiced all season, and the same is true of studying. Everyone studies best in his or her own way, but to study efficiently you need to find a routine that works best for you and stick to it. That may mean finding a place at the library that's quiet to sit and read for a few hours, or making sure you have a spot equipped with enough water, snacks, and books so you're not constantly getting up in search of sustenance. Studies have shown that even changing the room you study in can be hugely beneficial to retaining information, so switch it up and prepare to be amazed.

By consciously honing my study skills, I pave the way to success brick by brick.

HOW TO STUDY *better*

How do you actually hit the books and remember everything you packed into your cranium? The key is being mindful of your time. Research has shown that cramming at the last minute is a really terrible way to study, since anxiety and stress make it harder for your brain to hold on to facts. Instead, write out a schedule for yourself and stick to it. If you're going to study biology every night for the week leading up to your test, plan out *what* you'll study each night so you have a plan from the start. Another important thing? Remember to reward yourself with the occasional break so you can give your mind a breather. When it comes time to take your test, take a few deep breaths before starting and remind yourself—you've got this.

Being smart about my studying
will help me be wiser, too.

LAST-MINUTE *study* TIPS

You've got a big test coming up but you realize that you've spent more time on social media over the past few weeks than you have studying for that all-important test. There's no need to panic, though. Instead of endlessly flipping through test questions at the eleventh hour, try refocusing your negative energy on something positive. Breathe deeply and think about how best to spend the time remaining before the test. Think about productive ways to gather and remember information. Take time to center yourself and come up with a plan of attack that will leave you ready and refreshed come test day. That could include studying with friends, making time for working out, getting a good night's sleep, or just being mindful about what your brain (and body!) is telling you as you're trying to remember Darwin's theory of evolution. Figuring out how your mind works will help you become a better studier to boot.

My brain is an extraordinary thing, and I will take time to discover it and utilize it to the best of my ability.

WHAT TO DO IF YOU *fail* A TEST

Sometimes the cards just stack up against you. Maybe you didn't understand or retain the subject matter (er, what is inorganic chemistry again? And which guy was the thirteenth president?) or you let procrastination get the best of you and frittered away the time before a test. Or maybe you even wrote down the test date wrong (hey, it happens!). Whatever the reason, acknowledge it and take responsibility. You'll have plenty of problems in life, but it's never a good strategy to blame outside influences for your mistakes. Breathe in and realize that one mistake does not define you. Breathe out and calm your mind, and resolve to work not just harder but better. A failed test isn't the end of the world, but it sure means that you need to re-evaluate the way you approach the subject matter. If you really just can't remember that Millard Fillmore was the thirteenth president, give yourself a break, then give yourself the chance to succeed. Maybe you can't make up that failed test, but ask yourself how you can improve for the next time.

I will not beat myself up over one failure, but instead look at it as a new opportunity to achieve something better than before.

A NEW APPROACH TO *choosing* A COLLEGE

There's more pressure than ever before on teens to start thinking early about their higher education. The college admissions process is more cutthroat than ever before, as is the competition for scholarships as students grapple with the ever-rising cost of education. And all of that translates into lots of stress for you—making sure you have the right extracurriculars (volunteering at ten different organizations in your spare time, overseeing the Model UN, becoming a master concert pianist and flautist), impeccable grades, hours of test prep classes and quizzes, and knockout letters of recommendation. Not only is the frenzy unsustainable, it's not healthy, since it means you're likely ignoring your actual preferred hobbies (maybe you want to take a pottery class or an art class, even if you know you eventually want to be a doctor or lawyer) and setting yourself up to burn out. Instead, focus on what kinds of things you want from a college (rigorous academics or good sports teams, for instance) and what reasonable things you can do to make yourself a good candidate. Everyone applies to Harvard. If that's your dream, go for it, but remember that it's about finding the best fit for you. Your college choice doesn't define you, and it's important to focus on not only becoming a better student in high school but a better person.

I acknowledge that the journey to college is a long one and will be stressful, but I'll use this pressure to my advantage, reminding myself constantly that I am more than the schools that accept me.

MOVING ON FROM A *college* REJECTION

So your applications are in and you're frantically checking the mail (or your e-mail) to see if you got into your dream school. Suddenly, there's the letter that starts out with, "Due to the overwhelming number of qualified applicants this year . . . ." You don't need to read any further—you didn't get in. But a rejection letter is far from the end of the world. It's understandable that you're disappointed, and it's okay to let yourself be sad for a while.

But obsessing over why you didn't get in or what you could have done better is a waste of your time—especially since you can't change anything. If the school really was the only place you could ever see yourself, talk to your parents or someone you trust about your other options (there are *always* options, even if it doesn't look like it now!). Maybe you take classes at another college and try transferring in the next year, using your good grades and excellent recommendations as proof you're just too good to pass up. The point is, there's no reason to freak out. A rejection from your top school isn't a rejection of *you*. And you probably have a whole list of schools that couldn't be happier to accept you.

Instead of obsessing over the things I cannot change, I will focus my energy on what I did well—just because one college turned me down doesn't mean I don't have other options.

BALANCING SCHOOL LIFE *and* NORMAL LIFE

School takes up not only a majority of your day, but also a majority of your life. You've probably been in school for more than a decade by now—countless hours spent with multiplication tables, textbooks, and science equipment. But while it's a huge part of your life right now, it's not always the biggest. You have a family outside of school—your mom, your dad, maybe siblings and cousins—as well as friends and acquaintances. Maybe you're involved at your church, synagogue, or mosque, and you volunteer at a soup kitchen some weekends. Yes, school is important, and doing well there is important, too. But you shouldn't put that in front of being a good son or daughter, and a good friend. Taking stock of the things that are important will help maintain perspective, which is essential for helping you ace not just school but life.

My life at school is not my whole life. By taking stock of the other parts of my life and making time for others, I can clearly gauge what is important.

WHAT TO DO IF YOU'RE *failing*

Everyone has trouble with one subject or another at some point. But struggling in school—or even failing at it—is not a qualifier of your self-worth, though it can obviously make you feel crummy about yourself. Remember this: Failing a test or getting a bad grade in a class is not an indicator of failure in *life*. Give yourself time to wallow, then come up with a new plan. Maybe starting a study group, hiring a tutor, or asking the teacher for extra help would help you start over. Things are never as hopeless as you may first believe.

Failure is a means to an end.
It helps me discover my
strengths—and weaknesses—
and ultimately helps me
become stronger.

WHAT TO DO IF YOU'RE *succeeding*

Maybe school comes easy to you and you're the kind of person who can ace a test without cracking open a single book (lucky you!). It's easy to get teachers to like you, and you know even before you get a term paper back that there's going to be a big, fat, red A on the cover. First off, it's great that you're doing well! And succeeding—whether it comes through a natural aptitude or good old-fashioned hard work—feels incredible. But make sure to take your success in stride. It's easy to get overconfident or smug about your academic achievements, which paradoxically can make you try less and do worse. If you think you don't need to study for a test and then you flunk it, you come off as lazy and arrogant. Take stock in your success, but remember that there's no "coasting" setting in life. Everything in life won't come as easily, and you'd be doing yourself a disservice by not pushing your- self, even when the going's good.

Success is something to celebrate, but it's not an excuse to coast. I'll continue to push myself to thrive, because the moment I stop is the moment I lose momentum.

MUSICAL ME: *mindfulness* WHILE YOU PLAY

There's something really great about playing an instrument, whether it's the flute, the cello, the drums, or a tambourine. It's not just about making noise (though your parents may argue that's all playing the drums really is); it's about being creative. Since a lot of instruments (like the trumpet or oboe) require certain breathing techniques, practicing your music is a natural way to practice being present. In fact, your band instructor has probably already told you about the importance of breathing at the right time, in tempo, on beat. Take that one step further and look at how you're sitting (or standing) when you play, how your fingers help you play the right notes, or how you shape your mouth around the mouthpiece to get that really great high note. And of course, don't just listen to yourself when you play. Make sure to hear how your part fits into the whole, thinking of your instrument as one part of a much larger masterpiece. Bravo! Bravo!

I use my breath and my creativity to connect to music and let the music flow through me, being present and open to all of the sounds and sensations.

GAME FACE: BEING MINDFUL IN *sports*

Playing a sport requires coordination, discipline, and a dash of fear-lessness. Believe it or not, you can do all that *and* still be mindful. And don't think that being mindful means you have to let the other team win. This is more about tapping into the current moment and being aware of what your body can and can't do. If you're a runner, maybe that means being aware of when you can push yourself one iota more. Or it could mean simply being in the present moment of a football game and not thinking back to the previous play where you fumbled the ball. A major sports study found that athletes who utilize mindful-ness often are better performers and show better control in and out of the sports arena, so tap into your inner calm and prepare for some great things.

Keeping my mind in the game,
I focus on my success.

EMBRACE THE *unknown*

From the moment you learned how to talk, people have probably been asking what you want to be when you grow up. You might have said "Firefighter!" or "Marine biologist!" as a default answer, as both seem really cool and fun. Some people simply know from Day One that they want to be a doctor or an actor or a pastry chef, but for most of us, figuring out how you want to spend the rest of your life is something of a many-layered puzzle. The beauty of it is you're still young and you have time to figure out your interests and ambitions. True, middle school and high school require a lot of basic classes, but use your curiosity and passion to dig deeper. If you unexpectedly love biology, talk to the teacher to find out what kinds of books to read to find out more. Or maybe your school offers extracurricular clubs that let you explore your interests outside of class. A bit of a Francophile? Join your school's French Club or start your own. It could open doors for you down the line that you wouldn't have otherwise known. The point is, there's a great deal of comfort in not knowing exactly what you want to be when you grow up, because that means you're exploring your options.

In uncertainty, there is comfort. My options—and my mind—are open to possibility.

HOW TO TAKE YOUR LIFE *one* STEP AT A TIME

Some of the best advice I ever got regarding my future was from a very wise college counselor: Think only of what you want to do next, and figure out how to do it. Don't try planning your entire life right here and now, because that'll drive you crazy. Maybe you want to try something out after college—maybe travel journalism or politics—but you don't know if it's a perfect fit for you, forever and ever. Is that a problem? Absolutely not! In this day and age, the majority of people don't stay at the same company—let alone the same field—for more than a few years at once. You're doing yourself a disservice by worrying about the minutiae of what your life *might* look like fifteen years from now. Best to spend your time exploring the next immediate step (scoring well on a test), followed by the next (applying to a great college), followed by the next (running for mayor)—*then* worry about becoming President of the United States.

Taking small steps one at a time,
I can climb mountains.

"PROMISE ME YOU'LL ALWAYS REMEMBER: YOU'RE BRAVER THAN YOU BELIEVE, AND STRONGER THAN YOU SEEM, AND SMARTER THAN YOU THINK."

—A.A. MILNE

BEING YOUR BEST: SELF-ESTEEM AND SELF-CARE

HOW TO *practice* SELF-CARE

If you've ever stayed up all night finishing a last-minute assignment or lost shuteye at a sleepover, you know that you're not at 100 percent the next day. Maybe you're sleepy, groggy, or just slow on the uptake. But when you get a good night's sleep, you're (usually) ready to take on the day. Taking care of your mental health is no different. If you ignore your emotions and feelings and don't process them or work out your issues, they'll make you feel downright lousy. Luckily, the power of mindfulness meditation can help you take the best care of yourself. Try starting with a five-minute breathing exercise every morning before you start getting ready for the day. Breathe. Relax. Think about all you hope to accomplish today and how you'll go about it. And smile.

This time in the early morning is my own—a wonderful way to focus my body and my mind to help me carry out my goals for today.

DO THE *write* THING: KEEPING A JOURNAL

Your moods and emotions are complex, made all the more confusing by a tsunami of hormones. Since they're bouncing around in your head all day, these moods and emotions can get mixed up, jumbled, and hard to process. That's why keeping a journal—even if it's just one where you write out the emotions you felt that particular day—is so important. If you want to write more, go ahead! Getting your thoughts down on paper is a fantastic way for you to process everything and work through things that are bothering you. An added bonus: It's so cathartic to spend time away from a screen, and, years later, a reminder that whatever problems you faced weren't, in fact, the end of the world.

Writing is a way to keep my thoughts organized and to track my progress.

WHAT'S GOING ON WITH YOUR *body*

If you've suffered through the awkwardness that is health class and been forced to watch old DVDs of afterschool specials, you know that your brain and your body are in the middle of a vast metamorphosis. Yeah, it's kind of weird, but it's also unavoidable and will turn (or has turned) you into a young man or woman, whether you like it or not. Mindfulness can help you in this inevitable journey. Be aware of how you feel every morning when you wake up. Are you suddenly all arms and legs and tripping over yourself? Does your brain feel fuzzy? Did your voice suddenly drop half an octave? Or maybe you're just feeling especially irritable or cranky, which could be due to some nifty new hormones coursing through your body. Tapping into the root of how you're feeling can help you (figuratively) balance yourself for the day ahead so you can (literally) take on the day.

My body is changing fast, and to best understand it I must connect my brain to my body, focusing on how each part of my person talks to the other part.

CELEBRATE HOW *amazing* YOUR BODY IS

There are billboards and ads everywhere telling you that you need to look and act a certain way. Catalogs show svelte, skinny models laughing on a beach or in a mountain lodge, dressed in perfectly coordinated clothes with glowing complexions and flawless makeup, or men with washboard abs who look like they stepped out of an action movie. With all of these mainstream messages reinforcing that you have to look a certain way, it can be hard to deal with reality and accept your body for what it is. Instead of constantly comparing yourself to ads, celebrate what your body can do for you—let you climb mountains, or fight off colds, or do cartwheels, or feel restful and refreshed after a good night's sleep. Remember, those ads and billboards showing models laughing in some field or at a gym only exist to sell you something. Your body is your own and isn't dictated by what someone else thinks it should be!

My body is my own. From my fingers to my toes, I am me, and I am greater than just the sum of my parts.

Love WHAT MAKES YOU UNIQUE

Feeling good about yourself has to come from inside of you. Being confident and smiley on the outside may convince your friends and family that everything's fine, but until you believe—*really* believe—that your body is unique and striking, you're stuck with a burden you shouldn't have to bear. When you look in the mirror, don't analyze what you dislike or focus on a part of yourself you might change if you could. Think beyond the idea that the only "acceptable" beautiful people are women who are blonde, tall, and thin, or men who are tall, toned, tanned, and strong, and accept your body—and everyone else's—for what it is. Negative self-speak is a slippery slope, and one that can cause a lot of pain. Instead, break yourself out of the cycle. Start thinking of all of your great traits—not just physical, but the things that make you uniquely you. Once you repeat those to yourself time and time again, the thoughts become a talisman against the pressures of the outside world.

I believe my body is unique
and beautiful, and I love _____.

*Think of three things you love about yourself or your body every time
you do this meditation—you may love the way your body is strong
and capable, that you're empathetic and kind, or the
way you get freckles when you've been out in the sun.*

LEARN TO *respect* YOUR BODY

When it comes to your body, you have the final say. Accepting, respecting, and loving your body and your shape, as well as being healthy in body and mind, are a top priority, one that starts with what foods you put in it and how much sleep you give it. As you do that, be sure that the choices you make about your body are in line with your values and what's best for your future. It's not just about what foods you eat; it's about how you take care of yourself on every level—making sure that you're smart about the choices ahead and have sought out ways to keep things you don't want to happen from happening. Your body, your choice.

All bodies are beautiful, including mine. I will treat it with the respect it deserves.

FEELING GOOD AT *any* SIZE

If you've ever gone shopping and felt supremely frustrated about the limited size options (jeans that don't come in tall or short, tops that mysteriously aren't made beyond a certain number, shoes that aren't wide enough or big enough), you're not alone. It can be especially hard if there's a certain style you just *have* to have but it doesn't come in your size. Your first reaction might be anger or shock—*Why can't they just make more diverse sizes?* Or it might be shame that you can't fit into the limited options offered at this one store. Neither of these thoughts is at all constructive. Instead, find clothes that fit your body regardless of the label size (who cares what the labels say, anyway?) and that show your personality. Remember that stressing out about your size does more harm than good, and the focus should never be about "success" versus "failure." Look at each day as a fresh start, and if getting healthier or losing weight is one of your goals, think positively about how you will reach them in a productive, healthful way.

The same goes for how you treat others. Just as you don't judge yourself, judging other people on their looks is petty (and makes you miss out on their other lovely traits). Judging people by their character is a much better way to live your life, and people will respect and admire you for it.

I am more than the label in my clothes or the number on my scale. I feel beautiful when _____, and feel powerful when _____.

FOOD FOR THOUGHT: *mindful* EATING

Think of this scenario—you're at the movies with a group of friends and you've decided to partake of the great joy of movie theaters—the concession stand. Maybe you split some snacks like a 64-ounce tub of popcorn, a giant bag of gummy bears, and a soda. By the end of the first half of the movie, your friend reaches over to get some of the popcorn you've been hoarding and you find that somehow you ate the entire bag without thinking about it. When you don't think about what you put into your body, it's easy to shovel whatever's in front of you into your mouth. That's an awful way to eat, not least because you end up feeling sick to your stomach after eating a metric ton of buttered popcorn. Mindful eating—much like mindfulness itself—is about being present. You can do this any number of ways, like taking smaller bites and spending more time chewing while focusing on the texture and taste of the food. It's also asking yourself if you're truly hungry or simply bored, so you don't snack mindlessly. It's a small change that can help you be not only healthier but happier.

What I put into my body is directly related to what I can get out of it. I will make an effort to savor every spoonful and be thankful for the food in front of me.

stay HYDRATED

Not all mindfulness has to be about some deep, spiritual awakening. It's also about the basics, like drinking water! Being mindful helps you be attuned to what your body's telling you. Your body could be protesting that you didn't give it enough sleep last night, or it could be holding a grudge from how hard you worked it during the last basketball game. Are you feeling lethargic? Have a headache? Experiencing digestive issues? You might just be thirsty. Make sure to drink plenty of water every day (doctors say around eight glasses). It's a simple task, but one that will keep you looking—and feeling—better for years to come.

By listening to my body,
I discern its needs.

MINDFULNESS ON *foot*

There's nothing like going for a long, relaxing walk, especially when the weather is great and there's a gentle breeze. Being mindful while you do it is easy—just focus on how each step feels as you transfer your weight from the ball of your foot to your other heel, right foot, left foot, repeat. Feel how your joints are responding and how your muscles gradually loosen up the longer you walk. Take in your surroundings, looking up at skyscrapers or trees, depending on where you are at the time. Let your mind wander where it will and get into a rhythm. Nobody says you can only be mindful when you're still. A walking meditation isn't just good for your mind—it's good for your whole body!

One foot, then the other.
Peace, then understanding.

REACH FOR THE *sky*:
TAKING TIME TO STRETCH

There's nothing more satisfying than taking a nice, long, luxurious stretch after being hunched over a desk for most of the day. But we're often so busy that it's hard to remember that our bodies need not only food and water to keep going strong but moments to literally decompress and unwind. Try this: Any time you've been sitting for more than an hour, stand up and stretch. Put your hands over your head, arch your back, twist your torso from side to side. Basically, do whatever feels good! Doing so not only keeps you loose and limber; it feels great and helps increase blood flow to your muscles. What's not to love about that?

Keeping my body elastic helps
me keep an open mind.

MINI MEDITATION:
mindfulness IN A MINUTE

There will be some days when you feel like you just can't get up early to practice mindfulness, or you're so busy that it's hard to find time during the day to be present. Not ideal, but it's understandable! When you feel pressed for time, simply do a quick check-in and remember your breathing. Are you breathing deeply or are your breaths shallow? Are you holding tension in your face, neck, shoulders, or belly? Give yourself ten to fifteen seconds to breathe deeply and rotate your shoulders back, thinking about the present moment. It's like a small reset button that'll help you stay focused and centered. Still don't think you've got that kind of time? It only takes fifteen seconds to take and upload a selfie, tweet at your favorite celebrity, or make plans with friends via text. What are you waiting for? Time's a-wasting!

Using my breath to keep me centered, I can quickly refocus my energy.

THE *waiting* GAME

The last time you were stuck in a long line, what did you do? Tap your foot impatiently? Bury your head in your smartphone? Sigh loudly over the grand injustice of it all? While those all may be ways to pass the time, they're not exactly productive. Sure, it's tempting to get some extra time in on Snapchat, but this is a key opportunity to really challenge yourself to be present. Take in everything around you; observe the other people in the line and their body language. Imagine what their lives might be like. Do they go home and secretly write novels or practice jiu jitsu? Think of what sounds you're hearing. And, of course, focus on your breathing. Notice how much more chill you feel when you take a deep breath. It won't help the line move any more quickly, but changing your perspective about an inevitable nuisance is just as important as making it to the front of the line.

Waiting in line is the perfect opportunity to be present. When I focus on what I see, hear, and feel, I can feel my perspective shift.

FINDING MINDFULNESS IN YOUR
morning ROUTINE

Getting ready every day can be a drag. Brushing your teeth, combing your hair, and that whole annoying business of showering—it's impossible to multitask while doing that stuff, right? Nope! Aside from wanting to look (and smell) your best, the time you spend getting ready is prime time to be aware of everything you're doing. If you usually zone out while brushing your pearly whites in the morning, instead try thinking of all the ways you're helping yourself by having a sparkling smile—the least of which will mean fewer trips to the dentist. The goal here is simply focusing on the task at hand. Instead of whipping your comb through your hair in the morning like a madman, just focus on the act of brushing, not thinking of the ten other things you have to do to get ready this morning. What's the rush? Okay, well, you need to make sure you don't miss the bus. But beyond that, there's a lot of merit in diligence and focusing on personal hygiene.

Even when brushing my teeth or combing my hair, I pay attention to the task at hand.

FEEL *better* ON BLUE DAYS

If you live in a temperate climate with marked seasons, you've probably seen it all. Snowstorms. Blizzards. Nor'easters (if you're on the Eastern Seaboard). Heat waves. But the weather where you live is probably sunny more times than not (unless you live in Seattle or San Francisco). Sunny days are great because you get to go outside, go on a hike, or go for a swim, if the weather's warm enough. But without rain, you wouldn't appreciate the sunshine nearly as much (just ask anyone from Southern California). In the same way, some days are just going to be dreary inside your brain. But you know what the great thing is? It's only temporary. When that day is done and over, you get to start a whole new day that carries the promise of being even better than the last. If you're bummed about something or just can't shake the feeling of the blues, try thinking of a happy memory or upcoming adventure. It could be looking forward to a spring break trip, or a really great memory of time with your family. Whatever it is, realize that it's okay to feel blue, but in time, the sun will come out from behind the clouds, and everything will be better than it is now.

There's nothing wrong with feeling blue. I know that clouds sometimes cover the sun, and there's beauty in that. There's comfort in knowing the clouds won't last forever.

FEEL *thankful* EVERY DAY

You've probably already heard about the importance of adopting an attitude of gratitude and focusing on the positive things in your life. But what does that even mean beyond a tired cliché? Isn't it enough when you're grateful for Thanksgiving dinner and the mounds of sweet potatoes and pumpkin pie that will soon be happily in your stomach? Well, not really. Thanksgiving is a good place to start for taking inventory of all the things for which you're thankful, but it's by no means the finish line. When you have an average day that's probably going to simply fade into the fabric of your life, remember to take stock—are you thankful for that text your friend sent you that made you feel special? What about when someone at lunch let you take the last slice of pizza? Small, seemingly inconsequential things are the threads of thankfulness, and gratitude for those small things can be practiced every day.

Good things are in my life every day, if I only take the time to look for them. Being thankful every day builds a lifestyle of gratitude.

COUNT YOUR *blessings*

Some days, things are just going great. You aced a test, had a fabulous date, or received some good news. That's *fantastic*! And you should celebrate accordingly. Not everyone in the world is so lucky. There are people without homes, without families, without food or warm clothes. When you constantly assess all these wonderful moments in your life, you begin to acknowledge that, yeah, you're probably really #blessed. This perspective can help you see the world and those around you in a different light.

Every day is a chance anew
to feel thankful, happy, and
fulfilled by all the things
that are in my life.

HOPES *and* FEARS: DEALING WITH ANXIETY

Now more than ever there are a thousand things vying for your attention, and beyond this, a desire to be good at those things. Not only that, but the future feels uncertain as you change, your friends change, and life around you goes from the familiar to the unknown. Maybe you don't know where you want to go to college or what you want to do with the rest of your time in middle school and high school—and beyond. Maybe you don't even know what you want to do next week. Some anxiety problems can be sorted out easily with simple changes in diet or adding exercise to your routine. But others need more thought and care (and sometimes, professional help from a doctor or therapist). It's okay not to have all of the answers or to not feel like you know everything about your future. It's okay to worry, because that also helps you more earnestly find a solution to the problem. Anxiety can be greatly lessened by being mindful.

I will not let my anxiety get the best of me. There are parts of my life that may be uncertain or unclear, but I will embrace those as challenges and opportunities to grow stronger.

STRESS HURTS:
DEALING WITH ANXIETY'S *physical* SIDE

Let's talk about the physical manifestations of anxiety. There are a lot, and it can really affect your well-being and quality of life. It could be a sick, dropping feeling in the pit of your stomach when you forgot to study for a test, cold sweats when you realize you left your term paper sitting on your desk at home, problems sleeping because you're anxious about a friend issue, and so on. Breathing exercises can do wonders to help you calm down and re-center yourself. But you can also try something else that's physical to help work through the tension. Find something that relaxes and rejuvenates you, whether that's going on a walk around your neighborhood or cooking a meal for your family. Or maybe you just want to pamper yourself with a warm bath that helps your muscles relax. All of these are great ways to help manage the physical stresses of being—well—stressed. And during all of these exercises, remind yourself that this is just another problem to be solved, not a chaos-inducing situation to avoid.

Anxiety affects not only my mind but my body, too. Being mindful, I will take care of my whole person in a way that helps me reduce stress and improve my well-being.

ANGER: *learning* TO LET GO OF ANGER

Being angry isn't as simple as just, say, being hungry. Where the latter is easily solved with a sandwich and an apple, the former is comprised of a whole range of emotions, spanning from being mildly annoyed at something, to frustration, to full-blown blinding rage that makes it hard to think. But let's be clear: Being angry isn't wrong, because physiologically it's causing your important "fight or flight" response to kick in. Plus, sometimes you can channel your anger in a healthy way, like standing up for what's right in the face of adversity. But when you're always in a rage, stomping around feeling like the world has wronged you, it's unhealthy and a poor use of your time. What does your anger accomplish beyond that physiological response? Try to let go of the situation that made you livid in the first place and look ahead to the future. That doesn't mean that you condone someone's bad behavior, but it does mean you're not going to be connected to it any longer. Imagine that the anger is tied to you with strings. Cut those strings and free yourself.

I harbor a quiet peace inside. Learning to let go of my anger, I'm not weighed down by the past.

GREEN-EYED MONSTER:
DEALING WITH *jealousy*

When I was in tenth grade, a classmate showed up with the best new designer handbag. The brown leather was buttery soft and supple and smelled amazing, and she proudly showed it off to all of her fellow cheerleaders (she was, of course, the captain). I remember how jealous I was of her bag and the fact that she was so pretty and popular, with beautiful straight blonde hair. I even wrote some pretty nasty things about her in my journal. But looking back on it, I missed an opportunity to see past the fact that she had something I desperately wanted, and to make a real friend who liked the same things I did. Jealousy can do that to you—make you feel like there are angry hornets in your stomach and ants crawling on your skin. But jealousy is petty, and it really only breeds ill will and bitterness. What was I really jealous of? The attention? The fact that she was a cheerleader? I think in a way I had built her up so much and thought that since she came from a wealthy family her life was simply easier. Of course, that's not the case, and being mindful of your circumstances (and being thankful!) is the only way to protect yourself against this ugly green-eyed monster.

The opposites of jealousy are contentment and calm. When I feel jealous about something or someone, I will let calmness and contentment wash over me, constantly being thankful for what I do have.

build SELF-CONFIDENCE

Have you ever heard the phrase "fake it until you make it"? Think of how many people have used this idea in the course of history. Do you think kings and presidents and multiplatinum singers have been oozing self-confidence from Day One? No way! They've learned to have confidence in themselves and their abilities. Lucky for you, it's something that can be learned (and, yes, faked until you believe it). Here are two major tips for this. The first is learning to stop the negative self-talk. If you failed at something, don't be down on yourself. It's okay not to succeed, and hey, you'll just do better on the next one. The other is holding yourself tall, pulling your shoulders back, and smiling. Most people wouldn't believe that someone shuffling around with sad, sloped shoulders and a grimace is simply saturated in self-confidence, but they would believe that someone with a genuine smile and good posture has some special secret. That secret is to sometimes believe that you believe it, and soon enough, that turns into believing it outright.

Head up, shoulders back,
smile on: My secret weapons
for self-confidence.

HOW TO *deal* WITH BULLIES

Every school has them. The group of guys who picks on the shrimpy nerd. The gaggle of mean girls who make you feel bad about your clothes or your hair. Or that person who always makes a snarky comment on your Instagram posts. Bullies are, sadly, something you'll probably have to deal with (or have dealt with) many times over in your life. And while all fifty states have laws (and many others have both laws and policy) against it, bullying remains a constant problem.

Mindfulness can really help both parties in this situation. Take time to process and mitigate your emotions, no matter which side you're on (everyone makes mistakes and even the best of us might temporarily play the role of bully, as much as we hate to admit it). How, as the victim, does bullying make you feel? How, as the bully, do you feel when you say something mean or derogatory? Are you even aware you're making others angry or sad? Using the techniques in this book can help you form a barrier against criticism and bullying, and help you react more positively to challenging situations.

And, of course, it's extremely important to tell a parent or teacher that you're being bullied. When you take away your bully's power to make you feel less than you are, you're the true victor.

I am strong; I am courageous. I will let words of hate and ignorance trickle through me without consequence, like water trickles through my hands.

IT'S *okay* TO BE SHY

If someone has ever called on you in a public situation (whether in class or at a birthday party or an event) and you found yourself shrinking into your seat hoping to vanish, congratulations, you're shy! First off, don't think of shyness as a problem to be fixed—it isn't a fatal flaw or even something for which you should judge yourself. It is, after all, a part of who you are. Instead of beating yourself up over why you didn't speak to that cute girl (or guy!) at a party, think of the situation without judgment, and ask yourself what really defines you. We'll give you a hint—it's not your shyness or being introverted. On the flip side, you can use your self-awareness to help you assess social situations. What's so scary about talking to your crush, really? Try acting out the scene in your head and mustering the confidence you've gained from your meditation practice. Take a deep breath, relax, and smile. You're ready.

Without judgment or opinions,
I accept myself for who I am.

"LIFE CAN ONLY
BE UNDERSTOOD
BACKWARDS; BUT IT MUST
BE LIVED FORWARDS."

—SØREN KIERKEGAARD

NEW VIEW,
NEW YOU!
BEING BRAVE IN A
CHANGING WORLD

APPROVAL MATRIX:
stop LOOKING, *start* BEING

The name of the game in middle school and high school is trying to fit in. So many movies and TV shows deal with kids in school trying to do just that, with each of the characters looking—on some level—for the simple act of approval. In some situations, they desperately want validation; others seem like they don't really care, but deep down it's a driving force. Here's the thing, though. The characters always find out at the end that (spoiler alert!) they didn't need approval from their peers at all because they were special and unique to begin with. Looking for approval will only leave you sad and lonely. Instead, focus your energy on being the best possible person you can be—kind, loving, caring, energetic, weird, quirky, or whatever, and help those who also may feel isolated or crave approval. And save the drama for the silver screen.

Rather than waste my energy on seeking validation, I'll better use my time to be a better person and help others that I sense are struggling.

OVERCOMING *fear*-BASED THINKING

Maybe you're a naturally anxious person. Instead of enjoying a road trip with your family, your mind is drawn instead to worry about how cramped the family minivan feels or how icy the roads are and how you'll definitely, probably, maybe get in a horrible crash. Life can be paralyzing in its wealth of unknowns. Our bodies have developed fear as a primal response to keep us alive and safe from *perceived* danger, whether or not the danger is actually real. Fear-based thinking is problematic not only because it doesn't let you enjoy life the way you should, but because it's a vicious, unrelenting cycle. The more you allow your mind to entertain fear-based thoughts, the more your brain spirals them out of control into a ferocious Fear Monster that refuses to leave you alone. But your brain is malleable and can change itself, with some help from you. How, though? You could practice deep-breathing exercises to calm yourself. Simply asking yourself *why* you're afraid or fearful can help separate perceived threats from actual threats. Think about how you would feel if fear wasn't present in your life, and meditate on that. Little by little, you can help yourself go from a state of fear to one of calm.

Easing my fears, I become calm.
I allow myself to be present and
free of toxic thoughts.

GET TO SLEEP *faster*

Ever had one of those nights (or many of them) where you're just toss-ing and turning, thoughts racing, and you just can't get to sleep no matter how many thousands of sheep you try to count? We've all been there. But even in bouts of insomnia, being present can help you drift off into dreamland. This is another time to focus on your breathing, inhaling deeply, holding for a few seconds, and letting it go. There are many specific methods to try, but Dr. Andrew Weil's is, in my opinion, one of the best. He's a Harvard-trained physician who came up with the 4-7-8 technique. Here's how it works: Breathe in for four counts, hold for seven, and slowly breathe out for eight. When done continually over a few minutes, your body will naturally calm itself and release any ten-sions you might have. And since you're focusing on your breathing—not your cares and concerns—you can drift away worry-free.

Using my breath, I ease my way into a deep, restful, and restorative sleep.

SLEEP *better*

There's a reason why "sleep like a baby" is such a popular phrase. When you've only just come into being, you literally don't have a care in the world beyond hunger, and maybe the hope that you'll get mashed pears over mushy peas for dinner. But as you grow up, cares weigh on you, creating anxiety and worry and making "sleeping like a baby" ever more difficult. Studies have shown that practicing mindfulness reduces stress. Not only that, but being present can help trigger what Harvard doctor Herbert Benson, the director emeritus of the Harvard-affiliated Benson-Henry Institute for Mind Body Medicine, calls the "relaxation response."

But what *is* the relaxation response, exactly? It's the opposite of the stress response, which causes your body to tense up and generally feel awful. Going to sleep because you're in such a state of worry-free bliss will yield a better night's rest than, say, collapsing into an exhausted heap after hours of fretting. Your cares and problems will probably still be there in the morning, but you can face the day better knowing that you've got the power (and the power reserves) to take them on.

I am calm and relaxed.

Repeat this over and over, slowly, focusing on this mantra until you fall asleep.

MINDFUL MORNINGS:
WAKING UP WITH *purpose*

Mornings can be painful. The alarm goes off *way* too early, you keep hitting the snooze button, and you end up rushing through your morning because you waited too long to get ready. But it doesn't have to be that way. When your alarm goes off, try lying in bed for a few moments, consciously feeling your breath and beginning to feel your body. Notice the position in which you've been sleeping; start wiggling your toes and slowly flexing your muscles. As you start to feel more awake, focus your energy to the task at hand—getting ready for the day—and how you'll tackle the obstacles before you. No guarantees that this will make you *like* mornings, but at least you'll be coming at them from a position of calm.

When my alarm rings, I remind myself to wake up with purpose, being mindful of my body and how I transition from sleeping life to waking life.

FINDING *downtime*

These days, everyone seems to have calendars full to the brim with activities. Interpretive dance practice on Mondays, tae kwon do lesson Tuesdays, volunteering at the animal shelter on Wednesdays, debate team practice after school on Thursdays, Fridays are four-hour study sessions, and on the weekends, it's babysitting or working at the local supermarket. While it's great to be busy, sometimes we put way too much pressure on ourselves to do it all.

There's something to be said about gracefully being able to say no to an activity or event and giving yourself time to, well, relax and be a teenager! There's so much emphasis about academic and extra-curricular performance, but remember—you're your best self when you give yourself time to recharge and refill the well. Read a book (for fun!). Go to the movies or go ice skating. Or just give yourself permission to do nothing at all. Not everything is about a means to an end, and having a reminder to pace yourself is priceless.

Rest, recharge, rejoice. Not everything is about getting ahead or competing.

DO *more* BY DOING *less*

Do you try to do a bunch of tasks at once, since that is ostensibly what makes you the most productive? Doing homework while listening to a podcast while checking Facebook lets you do all three, right? Not so fast.

Conventional wisdom calls these collected activities "multitasking," but in realistic terms, it's more like trying to spin a dozen plates on sticks and keeping them all from falling and shattering on the ground. Mindfulness is the rejection of the idea that you have to do it all and all at once. Remind yourself that you can actually get more done by focusing on one task first (say, your history homework) versus bouncing from thing to thing and having to reorient yourself to the War of 1812 each time you go back to the history book. Sure, it takes discipline, but your brain (and your report card) will thank you.

The task in front of me is my task at hand, and I give it my undivided attention.

HOW TO UNPLUG *and* RELAX

Let's say you're lucky enough to be on spring break somewhere on a beach or up in the mountains. But instead of soaking up the sun or hitting the slopes, you're worried about finding the perfect Instagram shot or keeping up with the latest on Snapchat. It's easy to think that life will go on without you—like a train—if you somehow miss a post, but that just isn't true. Learning to detox from your phone/computer/ smartwatch/of-the-moment gadget isn't just healthy; it's a necessity for your own mental well-being. Sure, it's fun to catch up with friends and share the choice picture or two from your boating excursion. But try thinking of how you're feeling in the moment of the vacation. Take in the sights and smells of the beach. Hear the gulls crying and the surf crashing on the waves, and the vendors calling out, selling coco-nut water or churros. Being on social media by default takes you away from wherever you are. So try just being present. I promise, Facebook will be there when you come back from your trip.

I put down my phone and
use my senses to experience
what's around me.

NO OFF SWITCH: *constantly* BEING ON

Odds are you probably don't remember a time in your life without smartphones, and you had figured out all the bells and whistles of the latest iPhone before your parents could even decipher how to turn the thing on. You're probably a whiz at finding the best Instagram filter and scan Twitter in your downtime, but one thing you probably don't use is that little button on the top of your phone. That, you see, is the switch to turn it off. But most teens simply don't. It's your gathering space and social connector, and if you cut yourself off, what else is there? Despite what you might feel, sometimes it's good not to be reachable by friends (but it's important to always be available for calls and texts from your parents). Take a walk and leave your phone behind, or grab a coffee with a friend and power down your phone. You—and your device—deserve a break.

Just like a car engine isn't always meant to be on, neither is my phone. I will consciously and willingly disconnect so as to connect with people and things.

ON *being* ENOUGH

Scrolling through your Facebook feed, it's easy to think that everyone else has a much better life than you. Aiden just got a new gaming console. Mark scored tickets to the World Series. And Ellie's parents are taking her to Europe next month to visit relatives. Meanwhile, you're stuck sitting at home with nothing new or exciting going on. It's so, so easy to tie your self-worth into what you see on your screen, but that's far from the truth. While it may seem like Aiden and Ellie have it made, what they're not posting is probably more telling—parents fighting, money problems, and beyond. You are more than your newsfeed, and even though you may not be jetting to Belgium anytime soon, you are enough.

Deriving contentment from within and blocking out what's outside, I know that I am enough.

overcoming #FOMO

FOMO, or the "fear of missing out," isn't unique to the age of Twitter, Facebook, Instagram, and Snapchat. For generations before, people still invited some people to parties and not others, only now there's pictorial proof that you weren't there. At its root, the fear of missing out stems from the idea that this party, this concert, this show, this event will be the best thing *ever* and that if you don't go, you'll regret it forever. Sure, there are some things you shouldn't miss (like your cousin's wedding or a best friend's birthday party, for instance), but mindfulness is about assessing how you feel in the present moment. If you'd prefer to spend a Friday night in reading a book rather than going to a party, do it. Don't think about what you *might* miss by not going, but rather what you'll gain by staying. Use FOMO to your advantage by thinking of why exactly you're afraid to miss out on this thing, and consider it an opportunity to grow.

When I focus on what I'm missing, I fail to focus on what I have.

EMBRACING #YOLO (*well,* SORT OF)

YOLO, the acronym for "you only live once," is a no-holds-barred rallying cry similar to *carpe diem*, or seize the day. But while YOLO (and YOLO-ing) has been proliferated and parodied to the point of saturation or used as a catch-all for bad behavior, there is something to glean from the real philosophy behind it. At its core, YOLO-ing is about seizing an opportunity or doing something that you otherwise wouldn't when you take fear and regret out of the picture. What would you do if you lived your life without regrets? Maybe you would try to repair a friendship that's fallen to the wayside or reach out to someone in a different social circle without fear of rejection or mockery. When you calmly think about life's potential, fear and regret are placed on the backburner.

Focusing on the here and now, I leave regrets behind and embrace the richness that life has to offer.

LOGGING ON AND STAYING *safe*

So much of our lives take place online these days. You can order gro-
ceries online. You can hang out with friends online. You're probably
expected to do a lot of your homework online, too. But as easy and
as effortless as this all seems, there are dangers to it all. Just like you
wouldn't try to drive for the first time on a twelve-lane expressway,
you shouldn't delve into the fast lane of the Internet before you know
what you're doing. Information is so easy to transmit these days, and
it's all too easy to post compromising information—like a picture of
your house with the address clearly visible, or a part of your body
that's private—online for the world to see. Next time, before you post
something, take a minute to ask yourself, "Do I need to post this?
What's the benefit of doing it? And will anyone—including me—get
hurt by it?" If any of those answers are "yes," that photo or text does
not belong online.

My actions online should be meticulous and measured. Thinking before acting is the best way to keep myself and those around me safe.

#NOFILTER: *who* YOU ARE ONLINE

Social media is a big part of life nowadays, whether you like it or not. Companies hire bloggers and "influencers" on social media channels to promote their fantasy lifestyles to sell things like jeans or dresses or sports drinks. Friends' faces, meanwhile, are filtered to extremes, so as not to show a single pore or blemish, and makeup companies have started marketing "filter" makeup for the same reason. And Facebook posts are often edited or selective to show only the good and the humblebrags. The larger message? That your online persona should be flawless, and your life curated and perfect. But that's far from the truth. Life is messy—and often hard. And while it's probably not in your best interest to write about every hardship in your life on a public or semi-public forum like Facebook, it's good to be honest and not sugarcoat your life. If something is tough, go to a friend, a parent, an aunt, or a cousin, or explore your feelings offline. And when you do post online, do so as the best, most genuine you.

Instead of making it appear like my life is something it's not, I'll be genuine and courageous.

ON BEING *more* THAN YOUR NUMBERS

The other day, I was riding the subway and heard two young girls poring over each other's Instagram accounts. "How many followers do you have?" one asked. "Only 300," the other said, sounding dejected. "Why, how many do you have?" The other girl responded with a five-digit number, and I watched as the first girl sat back in the subway car, looking deflated. It's easy to get tied up in numbers—how many people you follow, how many follow you, how many likes or comments you get. But think of how many of those people you actually interact with in a real way. If you think of how many you interact with on a daily basis, the number is probably smaller still.

So why does it really matter that you have 10,000 followers on Instagram? How many of those people would you confide in if you're having a crisis? Instead, take stock of the richness of your friendships—these are the people who are there for you, through thick or thin. True, the number might not be all that impressive to the casual observer, but wouldn't you rather have a handful of great friends than an army of people who only "like" you?

The richness of my friendships—
not their numbers—helps shape
my self-worth.

USING YOUR *Vacation* WISELY

After months of anguished waiting and counting down the days, it's finally here! Summer vacation! Papers and tests and heavy backpacks are suddenly swapped for flip-flops and beach towels. But hang on just a second. Even if you have the luxury of a summer free of obligations like work or summer school, you shouldn't just fritter away your days because that can lead to—you guessed it—regret come September. Think of the fable of the grasshopper and the ants. The ants worked all summer because they knew they needed a stocked larder for the coming winter. The grasshopper, meanwhile, was content to play his fiddle while the sun shone, and was out of luck when the first snow came.

Plant your seeds early by thinking of ways to give back and enrich yourself. Maybe it's volunteering a day or two a week at an animal shelter, or helping out with your library's summer reading program. Or maybe pick up a few odd jobs around the neighborhood and earn a little extra spending money. An active mind is a healthy one, and though it may seem like unnecessary work, the last thing you want to do is end up like that poor old grasshopper. Hop to it!

Spending my summer improving myself and the things around me is anything but a bummer.

SHIFTING GEARS: THE *next* TEN YEARS

Want to blow your mind? Think of where you'll be in the next ten years. You'll probably be graduating college—or will be a recent college grad—and thinking about the next steps. Getting your first internship. Landing a job, or even a career. Figuring out what city you'll call home. And then, maybe traveling the world, settling down and getting married, inventing something, writing a book, or any iteration of those things.

That's a lot of changes—big, huge changes!—from sitting in algebra class and doodling in your notebook. Sure, it can be scary to think about, but it's also pretty exciting! You've probably thought a little (or maybe even a lot) about what you want to do after high school, but now's the time to make a habit of really digging into your interests. Yes, it's a little paradoxical to be talking about using mindfulness—which is rooted in the present and the here and now—to chart out your future ambitions and hopes, but look at it as more inner exploring. Asking yourself "Who am I?" and "What do I want to do with my future?" can help you carve out a better picture of where you'll be in a decade.

Looking inward, I can achieve greatness. Looking outward, I plan my steps.

KNOWLEDGE *and* COLLEGE

It may seem light years away, but the truth is, if you haven't already, you'll soon be getting pamphlets in the mail (or by e-mail) and making visits to the quads, dining halls, and tree-lined streets of college campuses. And, with more and more pressure on you, the prospective student, to get into an excellent college so you can lock down an excellent career, that's a lot of stress. Maybe your parents are pushing hard for you to get straight As on your report card, or pushing you into a bevy of extracurricular activities to look good for the Harvard admissions board. It's true that no matter what, looking at and applying to colleges will be stressful, but there's no need for that decision to hover over your head like a menacing rain cloud.

Try approaching each moment as it comes. As for the knowledge part of college in this meditation? It doesn't have to do with book smarts—it's all about knowing what you want out of a college experience. Maybe it's a big state school where you'll have 30,000 classmates. Or a tiny liberal arts college where you can pursue pottery with the best. Maybe it's Ivy League or bust. Whatever the case may be, use mindfulness as your secret weapon to take things one step at a time.

The biggest buildings start as a single brick. Keeping that in mind, I slowly build up my dreams for my future, staying true to myself.

FINDING OUT *your* PURPOSE

In case you hadn't noticed, your teenage years are some of the most difficult, hilarious, crazy, terrible, amazing ones. The hills are higher and the valleys lower than any other point in your life thus far. And factor into all of those changes the fact that you have tons of big decisions to make and it can be overwhelming, like trying to climb a Mount Everest made of quicksand. But by living your life in each moment, you can climb the mountain, step by step.

The same can be said about finding your purpose. Can you make the world a better place somehow? It's not like you'll wake up one day and—bam!—you know exactly who you are and what you want to do. It's a gradual process that takes time and thoughtfulness. By giving yourself time daily to think and assess, you're able to find a richer, deeper purpose than you would by just stumbling through at random.

Throughout the mountains and the valleys of life, I weave in and out, growing stronger in each step toward finding my purpose.

PURSUING *your* PASSION

Figuring out what you want to do with your life is kind of like the difference between being lost in the woods (barefoot, at night) and being able to use a GPS to see where you are and find your way out (with the best hiking boots and a powerful flashlight). You move confidently, swiftly, with a newfound sense of purpose and power. Finding your passion is similar. But it's not something that you can rush.

Whether your passion is studying the ocean floor or finding a cure for cancer, a passion often means long hours, tough choices, and a lot of grit, but it's worth it if it's what you really want to do. If you picture your life and can't see it without that aspect in it, call it a passion! Go confidently after your goal, realizing that with each step, you'll be in a better place than you were just a single step before.

Keeping myself firmly rooted in the present, I look forward to the challenges and triumphs the future years will bring through my purpose and my passion.